RUSSELL PUBLIC LIBRARY

S0-BAS-193

Joseph
Florida
32704

C-
975.9
Jy

DATE DUE

1998
MAY 1, 2012

DISCARDED

PRINTED IN U.S.A.

RUSSELL PUBLIC LIBRARY
32704

C -
9759
Jy

The United States

Florida

Paul Joseph
ABDO & Daughters

visit us at
www.abdopub.com

Published by Abdo & Daughters, 4940 Viking Drive, Suite 622, Edina, Minnesota 55435.
Copyright © 1998 by Abdo Consulting Group, Inc., Pentagon Tower, P.O. Box 36036,
Minneapolis, Minnesota 55435 USA. International copyrights reserved in all countries.
No part of this book may be reproduced in any form without written permission from the
publisher.

Printed in the United States.

Cover and Interior Photo credits: Peter Arnold, Inc., Super Stock, Archive

Edited by Lori Kinstad Pupeza
Contributing editor Brooke Henderson
Special thanks to our Checkerboard Kids—Teddy Borth, Kenny Abdo, Aisha Baker,
Gracie Hansen

All statistics taken from the 1990 census; The Rand McNally Discovery Atlas of The United
States.. Other Sources: Compton's Encyclopedia, 1997; *Florida*, Children's Press, Chicago,
1989.

Library of Congress Cataloging-in-Publication Data

Joseph, Paul, 1970-
     Florida / Paul Joseph.
     p. cm. -- (The United States)
     Includes Index.
     Summary: Surveys the people, geography, and history of the southern state
     known as the Sunshine State.
     ISBN 1-56239-853-9
     1. Florida--Juvenile literature. [1. Florida.] I. Title. II. Series: United States
     (Series)
     F311.3.J67   1997
     975.9--dc21
                                       97-10049
                                     CIP
                                     AC

Contents

Welcome to Florida

Florida is the playground for millions of sunseekers. The **Atlantic Ocean** is on the entire east coast of Florida. The **Gulf of Mexico** covers the west coast of the state.

Along these coasts are beaches filled with white sand. Because of the endless sand and sun, Florida is known as the Sunshine State!

Florida is also home to thousands of freshwater lakes. The Everglades National Park in South Florida is the largest **subtropical** wilderness in the United States. The Everglades is home to rare plants, birds, and animals.

Let's not forget where Mickey Mouse and his friends live. Disney World is the most popular vacation spot in the United States.

With all of the water, beaches, sporting events, animals, and parks, it is no wonder the Sunshine State is one of the most popular states to visit.

Andrews State Park, Panama City, Florida.

Fast Facts

FLORIDA

Capital City
Tallahassee (124,773 people)
Area
54,157 square miles
(140,266 sq km)
Population
13,003,362 people
Rank: 4th
Statehood
March 3, 1845
(27th state admitted)
Principal river
St. Johns River
Highest point
345 feet (105 m) in Walton
County
Largest City
Jacksonville (635,230 people)
Motto
In God We Trust
Song
"Old Folks at Home"
Famous People
James Weldon Johnson,
Ponce de León, Chris Evert,
Sidney Poitier, A. Philip
Randolph

*S*tate Flag

*O*range Blossom

*M*ockingbird

*P*almetto Palm

About Florida

The Sunshine State

Detail area

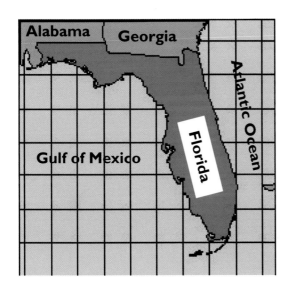

Alabama Georgia

Atlantic Ocean

Gulf of Mexico

Florida

FL

Florida's abbreviation

Borders: west (Gulf of Mexico, Alabama), north (Georgia, Alabama), east and south (Atlantic Ocean)

Nature's Treasures

Florida has balanced its **tourism** with farming and **industry**. It leads the country in the **production** of citrus fruits, such as oranges. And leads in processing citrus products, such as orange juice.

Florida is known for its beautiful sandy beaches. It is also known for its swampy Everglades. But it also has big pine forests that produce lumber, turpentine, rosin, and pulpwood.

The country's top producer of phosphate rock, which is used to make fertilizers, is Florida. Fertilizers make things grow, like the grass in your yard.

Florida's rolling grasslands help to feed the farmer's cattle. Its ocean water and lakes are home to about 700 different kinds of fish and shellfish.

Of course the weather is another treasure of Florida. It is sunny and hot most of the year. Most people visit the Sunshine State just because of the wonderful weather.

Oranges growing in the warm Florida sun.

Beginnings

In 1513, Juan Ponce de León was searching for the Fountain of Youth. Although he didn't exactly find it, he landed on North America. He claimed the land for his native **Spain** and called it La Florida, in honor of the Spanish Easter.

Spain controlled Florida until 1763 when they gave it up to England. During the **American Revolution**, Spain declared war on England. In 1783, England returned Florida to Spain.

By 1822, all of Florida became property of the United States. In 1845, Florida became the 27th state, and the city of Tallahassee was selected as the capital.

In the late 1800s railroads were built and this opened up Florida to the whole country. The state became a popular tourist resort and farming state.

After both World War I and II, people rushed to move into the Sunshine State. The boom continues today, with about 5,000 people per week moving to Florida.

Ponce de León in Florida, 1513.

B.C. to 1750

The Land and First Floridians

 When the first explorers landed in Florida it was mostly a barren land. It was covered with forests, swamps, and water.

 1513: Juan Ponce de León lands near present St. Augustine. He names the area La Florida and claims it for Spain.

 1750: The Creek Indians from Georgia migrate to Florida. Later, they become known as the **Seminoles**.

Florida

B.C. to 1750

Russell Public Library
1 ½ Main St.
P.O. Box 438
Russell, MA 01071
(413) 862-6221

1800s to 1950

Statehood and More

1845: Florida becomes 27th state on March 3.

1853: The University of Florida is founded in Gainesville.

1920-26: A Land boom brings many people to the state.

1947: The Everglades National Park is created.

1960 to Now

Present Day Florida

1961: The first astronauts from Cape Canaveral orbit around earth.

1990: A record-breaking 41 million people from around the world visit Florida.

1992: Hurricane Andrew, the costliest natural disaster in United States history, devastates parts of Florida.

1995-96: The Jacksonville Jaguars join the NFL and, in their second year, go to the AFC championship game.

1960 to Now

Florida's People

More than 13 million people live in Florida. Only California, New York, and Texas have more people. Floridians live in both large cities and small rural towns.

In 1821, there were about 5,000 **Seminoles** living in Florida. Most of the Native Americans were removed to the Oklahoma Territory. Some **descendants** remained and still live on the three **reservations** in southern Florida.

Many Floridian's native language is Spanish. Most come from either Cuba, Puerto Rico, or Mexico.

Some very famous people have made Florida their vacation home because of the wonderful weather. The Kennedy family has had an estate in West Palm Beach since the 1930s. Some of the Kennedys that have vacationed there include President John F. Kennedy, his brothers, Senators Robert and Teddy, and his son John, Jr.

Two of the greatest innovators in American history had vacation homes in Florida. Henry Ford and Thomas Edison both had homes in Fort Myers.

The singer Madonna, baseball player Jose Canseco, and millionaire Donald Trump each own homes in southern Florida.

Thomas Edison

President John F. Kennedy

Henry Ford

Splendid Cities

Jacksonville is the largest city in the state of Florida. Miami, the second largest city, is a winter resort that thousands of people visit each year. Tampa is an important port city on the Gulf coast. St. Petersburg is one of the country's great saltwater fishing resorts. Orlando is a very rich fruit-growing area. However, it is known more for being the most popular vacation city in the United States because of Disney World. It is also home to EPCOT Center, Sea World, Universal Studios Theme Park, and Cypress Gardens.

Tallahassee

Pensacola

Jacksonville

St. Augustine

Orlando

Tampa

St. Petersburg

Miami

Pensacola is the second oldest city in the state. It has a fine harbor on the Gulf and is the site of a naval air training station.

And St. Augustine, Florida, located on the northeast coast of the state, is the oldest city in the entire **continental** United States!

Miami Beach, Florida.

Florida's Land

Florida is a very long and thin state. It is the southern most **continental** state in the country. Florida is divided into five regions.

The Coastal Lowlands cover southern Florida and the entire coast. Pine forests cover much of this area, along with swamps and lakes. Lake Okeechobee, the largest lake in the southern United States, and the Everglades are a big part of this area.

The Central Highlands are the heart of the fruit-growing **industry**. It has broad plains, rolling hills, and thousands of lakes.

The Tallahassee Hills area has rolling hills of sand and clay. Corn and soybean fields and pecan groves circle this part of Florida. The Apalachicola River and Wakulla Springs run through this region.

The Marianna Lowlands is a flat and gently rolling area. The ground has limestone in it. The land has some ponds and small lakes, along with cypress trees. Its rich farming region's main crops are peanuts and soybeans.

The Western Highlands consist of valleys, streams, and rivers. The St. Johns River drains into the **Atlantic Ocean**. The Suwannee, Apalachicola, Chattahoochee, and Flint rivers all drain into the **Gulf of Mexico**.

The Everglades of Florida.

Florida at Play

Florida's sunshine, warmth, waters, and attractions not only bring millions of people, but also billions of dollars to the Sunshine State.

Florida has lots of fun things to do. The Kennedy Space Center and Spaceport U.S.A. at Cape Canaveral attract huge crowds.

Across the state are many animal exhibits. Wildlife, marine life, birds, reptiles, and trees can be seen at Sea World, Marineland, Seaquarium, and Busch Gardens.

Sporting activities are a big part of Florida. Besides water sports, there is no better place to golf than the Sunshine State. Florida is home to thousands of golf courses.

And if you like to watch sports, Florida provides the most action around. Professional teams include the Miami Dolphins, Tampa Bay Buccaneers, and Jacksonville Jaguars in football. The Miami Heat and Orlando Magic play basketball. The Florida Marlins play baseball there, along with many other professional baseball teams that play in the Grapefruit League during spring training.

Many people come to watch the space shuttle lift off.

Florida at Work

The people of the Sunshine State must work to make money. Many of the jobs deal with **tourism**, military, and service. Service is cooking and serving food, working in stores, hotels, or restaurants, and doing many other things for tourists who visit the state.

Many Floridians farm, mine, or fish. Today, Florida ranks first in the United States in **production** of oranges and grapefruit. Florida also produces a lot of honey.

The most grown vegetable crops are corn, peanuts, hay, and cotton. Fishermen catch and sell shrimp, lobsters, oysters, crabs, and many others.

Without the workers of Florida, the rest of the country would not have wonderful tourist attractions.

Without the farmers and fishermen in Florida, people all over America wouldn't have many of the fruits, vegetables, and seafood that they enjoy.

There are many things to do in Florida. Because of its weather, beaches, people, and many attractions, the Sunshine State is a great place to visit, live, work, and play.

Fishing is big business in Florida.

Fun Facts

•Florida has had only one state capital and it is Tallahassee.

•Florida is not a very tall state. Its highest point is in Walton County and it is 345 feet (105 meters). Its lowest point is at sea level.

•Forty-two bridges connect the strip of islands called the Florida Keys.

•Near Key Largo is America's first underwater park. You can take a ride on a glass bottomed boat and see 55 kinds of coral, many different tropical fish and sea creatures, and old wrecked ships.

Florida is surrounded by water on three sides.

Glossary

American Revolution: the war that gave the United States its independence from Great Britain.

Atlantic Ocean: one of a few large seas that surround continents. This one borders the entire east coast of the United States, including Florida.

Continental: the mainland of the United States, all of the states except Alaska and Hawaii.

Descendants: people who are related to others who lived a long time ago.

Gulf of Mexico: a large bay that borders most of the west coast of Florida.

Industry: a type of business.

Produce: to make; (**production**, the making of something).

Reservations: an area of land where Native Americans live, work, and have their own laws.

Seminoles: a group of Native Americans that lived in North America whose original members broke away from the Creek Native Americans and fled into Georgia and Florida.

Spain: an independent country in southeast Europe. Florida was first claimed by Spain.

Subtropical: the area just outside the tropical zone. The tropical zone is the land that lays along the equator, which is the hottest area on earth.

Tourism: an industry that serves people who are traveling for pleasure and visiting places of interest.

Internet Sites

Florida Info Link
http://orchid-isle.com/attr
Contains links to information on Florida's cities, weather, sports, museums, attractions, theme parks, camping, recreation and more.

Florida Kids
http://www.dos.state.fl.us/kids
This page is for you to join the Florida Department of State in its programs about Florida. We have pages on our museums, Florida folklife, archaeology, history, and more. We can lead you to information that will help with your Florida projects and essays. You can find out about the state flags, emblems, symbols, history, facts, famous people, place names, and lots more.

These sites are subject to change. Go to your favorite search engine and type in Florida for more sites.

PASS IT ON

Tell Others Something Special About Your State

To educate readers around the country, pass on interesting tips, places to see, history, and little unknown facts about the state you live in. We want to hear from you!

To get posted on ABDO & Daughters website E-mail us at "mystate@abdopub.com"

Index